Purpose is
BULLSH*T

Living Fully
Without Waiting for
a Bigger Reason

JUANISHA BYRD

ISBN: 979-8-218-72455-9

To my late father, Tony Williams—
whose memory lives on and whose love
inspires me every day.

TABLE OF CONTENTS

THE MYTH OF PURPOSE

You've heard it a thousand times: *"Find your purpose."* It's everywhere—on the lips of motivational speakers, plastered across social media, and sold in shiny packages by self-help gurus. The message is simple and seductive: *"Purpose" is the ultimate key to success, happiness, and fulfillment.* They tell us it will give us meaning, clarity, and direction, as though life's chaos will magically dissolve once we uncover this elusive secret.

It sounds promising, doesn't it? Like a golden key just waiting for you to discover it—a force so profound it will transform your entire existence and if you haven't found it yet, that's a problem, isn't it? You're lost, not trying hard enough, and wasting your potential and life.

What if everything you've been told about purpose is a lie? What if you don't need a purpose to truly thrive? What if pursuing purpose prevents you from living in the now, experiencing happiness and fulfillment now?

I believed that story for years. I chased purpose like my life depended on it. I climbed the ladder, checked the boxes, and crushed the goals, thinking each accomplishment would finally bring me that feeling of "arrival." But it never came. The more I achieved, the emptier I felt. I wasn't living; I was surviving—dragging myself forward, clinging to the hope that someday everything would "click" and life would finally make sense.

Chasing a mirage leaves you exhausted, pouring everything into something nonexistent. That was me, obsessed with one big "aha" moment—the clarity that would make me feel whole. Instead, I found only frustration, disappointment, and an insatiable emptiness that I couldn't escape.

Until one day, I stopped.

I stopped seeking purpose. I stopped waiting for some magical moment to save me. And in that stillness, I realized the truth: I didn't need a grand purpose to justify my existence. I didn't need to delay my happiness until I'd found some mythical "calling." I deserved to live fully—*right now*.

That's what this book is about.

This isn't an attack on ambition or self-discovery. Your dreams, goals, and passions matter deeply. But this *idea*—that your entire life should revolve around finding some singular purpose—is toxic. It's a lie that keeps us waiting, searching, and never satisfied. And it's time to let it go.

Let me be blunt: this concept of purpose? *It's bullshit*.

But here's the good news: you don't need a purpose to feel fulfilled. You can find joy, meaning, and freedom in the present moment—in the life you're already living right now. This book is your invitation to do exactly that.

Let's set expectations. This book is short, without fluff or filler. Life is too short for long explanations—and so is this book. If you're ready to break free from the myth of purpose and live fully in the now, you're in the right place.

CHAPTER 1

DECODING PURPOSE

History, Culture, and the Self-Help Revolution

Have you ever felt overwhelmed by the pressure to discover your purpose? It seems our entire existence often hinges on uncovering a grand, life-defining mission. This notion—that each of us must find some profound "why" behind our actions—has become a cornerstone of modern self-help. But is this framing constructive, or has it simply become another source of unnecessary pressure?

Ancient Perspectives

The concept of purpose is not new; it traces back to ancient philosophies addressing life's fundamental questions: Why are we here? What is the good life? In Aristotle's *Nicomachean Ethics*, the purpose is to define how humans achieve *eudaimonia*, or "flourishing." For Aristotle, the ultimate goal of life was to attain this by cultivating virtue, reason, and fulfilling one's potential. Thus, purpose is not about individual success or material gain but aligning with moral and intellectual excellence.

This idea resonates in many philosophical and spiritual traditions. In *The Analects of Confucius* and writings by Mencius and Xunzi, Confucianism emphasizes social harmony, moral duty, and ethical cultivation for a meaningful life. Confucius taught that individuals should cultivate virtue (*de*) through righteous actions and ethical principles like benevolence (*ren*), righteousness (*yi*), and propriety (*li*). A virtuous life is essential for fulfilling one's purpose.

Confucian philosophy also places great importance on filial piety (*xiao*)—the respect and care for one's family, particularly elders and ancestors. Living in alignment with family duties is considered a crucial part of a purposeful life. In addition, education and self-improvement are lifelong responsibilities. By learning, reflecting, and practicing ethical behavior, individuals develop wisdom (zhi)—not merely as knowledge accumulation, but as the discernment needed to act virtuously and promote social harmony. In this way, purpose is achieved through a continuous process of ethical cultivation, relational responsibility, and wise action.

Today's Philosophers

Fast forward to today, where contemporary self-help gurus, like Simon Sinek in *Start with Why*, urge us to "find our why" as the first step toward success and fulfillment. Rick Warren's *The Purpose-Driven Life* proclaims that life only begins when we understand our God-given mission. Media icons like Oprah Winfrey popularize the idea of discovering a "calling" that aligns passion, talent, and meaning. Together, these messages reinforce a singular idea: without a clear purpose, we are incomplete.

Modern self-help frequently portrays purpose as a personal journey toward fulfillment. However, this perspective is just one of many. Throughout various cultures and historical periods, the understanding of purpose has been influenced by differing values, often prioritizing the collective well-being or spiritual harmony rather than individual success.

Holistic, Non-Western Traditions

Eastern sources of philosophical wisdom tend to place the individual in the context of the whole: the family, the community, and the universe. In this schema, improving oneself is to align with the world and vice versa, not to discover a novel, unique ambition that one must achieve.

Consider the Indian concept of *dharma*. In Hindu philosophy, *dharma* represents a person's duty or role in life, tied to the social and cosmic order. Unlike the Western notion of purpose as something to "find," *dharma* is understood as inherent, defined by one's age, stage of life, and community. It evolves with circumstances and centers on balance, righteousness, and responsibility to others.

In Native American spirituality, purpose is deeply rooted in interconnectedness with people, nature, and the spiritual world. Life's meaning often emerges through relationships and contributions to collective well-being. Purpose here is less about individual success and more about maintaining harmony and honoring shared histories.

The Japanese concept of *ikigai* positions purpose at the intersection of personal passion, professional skill, societal need, and financial sustainability. Unlike self-help, which tends to isolate purpose as a singular "mission," *ikigai* recognizes it as multifaceted and fluid, adapting to life's shifting priorities and circumstances.

The philosophy of *Ubuntu* from Southern Africa challenges the individualistic view of modern self-help. It is summarized by the phrase, "I am because we are," capturing a profound understanding of purpose that is deeply rooted in community and interconnectedness.

Ubuntu emphasizes that an individual's purpose is not isolated but is found through relationships. In this framework, a person's worth and meaning are derived from their contributions to collective well-being and their interconnectedness with others. It celebrates the idea that our existence is intrinsically tied to the community and that we discover our purpose by fostering harmonious relationships, mutual respect, and communal responsibility.

Unlike Western, individualistic views that emphasize a unique personal mission, *Ubuntu* teaches that we cannot exist in isolation. It's not about pursuing a self-defined goal; it's about recognizing our connection to a greater whole and committing to the welfare of others. This perspective encourages seeking purpose through collective care and shared responsibilities, prioritizing interconnectedness over personal achievement.

In *Ubuntu*, purpose is not just about "finding" your mission; it's about recognizing your role in the community. Purpose is dynamic, shaped by interdependent relationships and mutual support. True purpose often comes from fostering well-being in others, not achieved alone but shared with those around us.

Context is Key

These cultural perspectives highlight an essential truth: purpose is not universal. It is shaped by the contexts in which we live, reflecting values that can contrast sharply with the modern obsession with productivity and achievement.

In the self-help industry, purpose is often framed as a North Star—a fixed, guiding light that promises fulfillment if only we can reach it. This metaphor is powerful, but it oversimplifies the complexities of purpose. It reduces a dynamic and deeply personal process to a checklist item or a branding exercise.

This framing can inspire or paralyze. It can provide clarity in chaos while also making purpose seem unattainable. If purpose is seen as singular or preordained, what happens if we fail to "find it"? What if we move forward and discover it wasn't the "right" step towards that purpose?

The reality is far more nuanced: purpose isn't something we stumble upon or unearth like buried treasure—it's something we create. It evolves alongside us, shaped by our experiences, values, and relationships.

Modern self-help portrays purpose as the ultimate destination—a singular mission to be discovered and pursued at all costs. However, this perspective fails to capture the complexity and fluidity of not only "purpose," but of ourselves. Human beings are adaptable and malleable creatures whose purpose reflects their current needs and contextual environments. As the cultural frameworks of *dharma*, Native American spirituality, *ikigai*, and *Ubuntu* remind us, purpose is not static or solitary. It represents a dynamic interplay between who we are, what we value, and how we connect with the world around us.

Rather than viewing purpose as a fixed destination, we can see it as an evolving process that grows and shifts with us. Purpose isn't a rigid blueprint; it's a flexible guide shaped by our choices and circumstances. Instead of pressuring ourselves to find the "one true purpose," we can explore, redefine, and adapt our sense of meaning throughout life's journey.

CHAPTER 2

THE MYTH OF PURPOSE

Who Sold Us This Idea?

oday, the concept of purpose is nearly inescapable. We're told we need it; and that without it, we're lost, drifting, or incomplete. It's pitched to us as the foundation of a fulfilling life, and a powerful reason for being that defines who we are and what we should do. But where did this idea originate? How did purpose evolve into a social expectation and a commercialized product?

To understand why we feel so much pressure to find purpose, we must examine the forces that promote it. Religion, self-help culture, corporate branding, and social media significantly embed purpose within society. These influences shape our obsession with purpose, turning it from private reflection into public demand—a principle we are urged to chase, relentlessly—even if it leaves us feeling more unfulfilled.

Religion and the Origins of Purpose

I grew up in a religious household, so I naturally understand that purpose has deep roots in spiritual beliefs, often intertwined with divine destiny or a "higher calling." In Christianity, for example, believers learn that God has a specific plan for each of us—a purpose that we are meant to discover and fulfill in order to serve Him. Scriptures like Jeremiah 29:11, "For I know the plans I have for you, plans to prosper you and not to harm you, plans to give you hope and a future," reinforce that our lives are shaped by a preordained purpose aligned with God's will. This sacred understanding of purpose gives many a strong sense of direction and significance, guiding their steps throughout life.

This belief is comforting for many, suggesting our lives are part of a larger divine plan—crafted with intention. It offers a sense of stability and assurance amidst the unpredictability. Knowing that everything happens for a reason, that even our struggles and setbacks are part of something bigger, provides a profound sense of hope. Religious doctrines worldwide resonate with this idea, implying that we are not here by accident, but to fulfill a unique role. For centuries, this belief has shaped people's understanding of who they are, where they belong, and their identity, belonging, and purpose. This spiritual understanding transcends personal ambitions, urging individuals to think beyond themselves and focus on the greater good.

Furthermore, the concept of purpose within religion serves as a profound coping mechanism. Stick with me on this: when life gets tough, and we face seemingly endless cycles of hardship, suffering, and loss, we often find comfort in knowing that these struggles are not meaningless. In religious contexts, we are frequently reminded that the difficult seasons of life—such as heartbreak, failure, grief, or any anguish we are battling—are all part of a greater plan. We need these experiences to unfold as they are meant to if our ultimate purpose is to be fulfilled. Even if you aren't personally religious, I'm sure someone you know has told you during a challenging time, "This is all happening for a reason; you will find purpose in this." It's the idea that there's meaning to be found in the pain and that the difficult experiences we go through are somehow integral to fulfilling our purpose.

However, as society has become more secular, our interpretation and pursuit of purpose have evolved. What was once viewed as a divine calling rooted in religious belief has shifted into a more personal quest for meaning. Without the clear guidance of a religious framework, purpose has become something individuals must discover and define for themselves. This shift has resulted in both freedom and pressure—freedom to determine purpose on our own terms and pressure to find that purpose amidst the complexities of life, often without a clear or structured roadmap to follow.

The Self-Help Industry: Purpose as a Product

Enter the self-help industry, which saw an opportunity to fill the gap created by society's shift away from religious and collective sources of meaning, ultimately redefining and repackaging purpose for a modern, consumer-driven audience. In recent decades, the self-help industry has exploded, capitalizing on people's insecurities, frustrations, and profound desire for meaning and fulfillment.

Books like *Find Your Why* by Simon Sinek and David Mead, *Man's Search for Meaning* by Viktor E. Frankl, and *The Purpose Driven Life* by Rick Warren have turned purpose into something almost scientific—a set of principles, strategies, and steps that, when followed, promise happiness, success, and fulfillment. What was once seen as a deeply personal, often spiritual quest has now been transformed into a universal pursuit that can be understood, packaged, and sold.

In *Find Your Why*, Sinek and Mead provide a guide for discovering purpose by identifying one's "why"—a core belief driving actions. The book frames purpose as a goal accessible through introspection and action, highlighting that clarity of purpose is vital for a fulfilling life. Similarly, in *Man's Search for Meaning*, Viktor Frankl, as a Holocaust survivor, argues that finding meaning is crucial to survival even in dire situations. Frankl's insights have become foundational in self-help, positioning purpose as a psychological necessity that helps us endure suffering and thrive in the face of adversity. Together, these works illustrate that purpose can be actively discovered and aligned with one's values and actions.

These books, countless seminars, motivational speakers, and life coaches deliver the same message: you must find your purpose to live a full life. Purpose, in their view, is no longer a quiet, internal compass; it's a necessity and a key ingredient in achieving a life of significance.

Purpose has become a product, a solution to modern problems like career dissatisfaction and low self-esteem. The self-help industry exploits our anxieties about meaning, presenting purpose as the missing piece that makes us whole, insisting that without it, we are incomplete. Like any marketed product, purpose remains elusive, driving us to seek the next book, seminar, or program. Thus, purpose has shifted from a sacred pursuit to a marketable commodity, sold as the ultimate answer for happiness.

This idea is immensely profitable, as it speaks to our deepest desires and fears. By framing purpose as something that can be found, achieved, or even bought, the self-help industry has created an enormous market for books, courses, workshops, coaching services, and retreats, each claiming to provide the key to unlocking our fullest potential. We're told that if we feel lost, unmotivated, or dissatisfied, it's because we haven't found our purpose yet.

And if we haven't found it, we haven't looked hard enough or used the right tools. The self-help industry promises to provide those tools for a price. But in doing so, it also nurtures a cycle of constant consumption, where our personal growth becomes dependent on external solutions rather than cultivating a more enduring sense of self-reflection or internal clarity.

Corporate Purpose as Identity

Self-help gurus aren't the only ones promoting purpose; corporations have embraced it too, forging deeper emotional connections with consumers. Companies now sell identities, lifestyles, alongside products. They aim to make us believe that aligning with their brand means buying a part of ourselves. Entering an Apple store isn't just about purchasing a gadget; it's about embracing the ethos of "thinking different" and a world that values innovation. Likewise, Nike's "Just Do It" urges us to see ourselves as athletes and individuals who defy limitations. These brands have transformed purpose into an aspirational concept woven into our daily lives.

Corporations have tapped into a fundamental human desire: the yearning to feel connected to something larger than ourselves, something that gives our lives meaning. In doing so, they position their brands as vehicles for this purpose—tools through which we can reflect our values and express our inner selves.

Mission statements from companies like Patagonia, which positions itself as a "crusader for environmental sustainability," or Ben & Jerry's, which champions "social justice," have shifted from corporate strategies to personal manifestos. By presenting themselves as aligned with causes that resonate deeply with the individual, these brands have become more than businesses—they have become movements. These almost sacred entities allow us to project our own purpose onto their products. This shift goes deeper than just selling a product—it's about offering us a sense of belonging and validation, a way to identify with something greater than ourselves.

This isn't just about consumerism; it's about filling the void that many of us feel in our fast-paced, and often disconnected lives. Brands like Patagonia and Ben & Jerry's recognize that we seek products making a meaningful difference. Aligning with these companies invites us into a community sharing our values, providing a sense of purpose and identity. Every purchase becomes a statement about who we are. In a world where finding purpose is challenging, these brands offer a way to feel good, even as we engage in the consumerism that can often feel hollow.

However, the impact of this corporate branding strategy runs deeper than we realize. While it gives us the emotional satisfaction of belonging to a larger cause, it often creates a subtle but powerful illusion: that purpose can be bought. That the simple act of purchasing the right product or aligning with the right brand can somehow make us better people. This emotional manipulation is a double-edged sword. While it offers temporary gratification, it risks overshadowing the actual, internal process of discovering personal purpose, often requiring introspection, sacrifice, and deeper engagement with the world around us.

So, we must ask: in a world where purpose has been commodified, are we genuinely fulfilling our deepest desires, or merely purchasing an identity that was never truly ours?

Social Media: The Performative Purpose

Finally, in the age of digital connection, social media has intensified the pressure not only to find purpose but also to showcase it publicly. Platforms such as Facebook, Instagram, and LinkedIn have turned the pursuit of purpose into a public performance, transforming it from something profoundly personal to something that must be curated and presented to the world.

Social media influencers, content creators, and thought leaders are building entire followings around their "missions," whether they advocate for mental health, social justice, or personal development. They claim to be "living their purpose." In doing so, they inadvertently raise the question: why haven't we found ours yet? Why does it seem like everyone around us is "living their best life," while we're left wondering where we fit into this narrative?

On social media, purpose is no longer something that quietly guides our actions or illuminates our values; it's something to be broadcast, validated, and admired. It's a form of signaling worth, passion, and success to a digital audience. We see carefully curated lives: people posting motivational quotes, documenting their personal growth, and sharing their milestones and achievements. We rarely see the struggles, doubts, or moments of silence in between.

The illusion of purpose on social media is polished and neatly packaged. Purpose is no longer an internal compass—it's a brand, an aesthetic, a performance. As we scroll through feeds of people fulfilled by their "higher callings," the message is clear: if you're not living with purpose and your life isn't visible and admired, you're doing it wrong. You're failing to meet an unspoken expectation.

This pressure creates a paradox. The more we strive to be "on purpose," the more we drift from our true selves. We become entangled in external validation, feeling emotionally drained, disconnected, and questioning: "Am I really living my purpose, or just performing for applause?" Social media, meant to connect us, amplifies our isolation. We constantly compare our authentic lives to the curated highlight reels of others, feeling inadequate and unsure of what's real. We're striving for the appearance of purpose, not *just* purpose itself.

Where Does That Leave Us, Then?

Purpose has shifted from an intrinsic principle to an outward expectation. Religion, self-help culture, corporate branding, and social media shape our obsession with finding and displaying purpose, leading to the pressure of having a clear reason for being. We believe purpose is essential for fulfillment; yet this pursuit often leaves us feeling fragmented. If purpose is vital for our well-being, why does chasing it exhaust us and make us feel inadequate? Why does it seem that the more we reach for it, the further it slips away?

As we consider these questions, it's crucial to acknowledge that the pursuit of purpose, like any other cultural ideal, is not something we've created entirely on our own. It has been sold to us through various societal systems, packaged in different forms, each promising us that we can have it if we just do enough, achieve enough, or look the part.

While the idea of purpose may feel empowering, it's important to ask: Who benefits from this endless chase, and at what cost to our well-being? I'm sure you can think of other ways the idea of purpose has been pushed upon us—some subtly, some with overwhelming force. Though I don't claim to know its exact origin, piecing together this larger picture helps us understand where the pressure to find purpose came from, who sold it to us, and—most importantly—whether we can reclaim our own definition of purpose, free from societal expectations.

CHAPTER 3

PURPOSE AS A PRIVILEGE

For many, purpose is portrayed as an essential pillar of a fulfilling life. Motivational speakers, self-help books, and social media influencers relentlessly hammer home the notion that everyone should have a unique purpose. But this widespread, feel-good narrative fails to acknowledge a glaring truth: the quest for purpose is often a luxury—a privilege afforded to those who already have their basic needs met, who don't have to worry about where their next meal is coming from, or who face systemic barriers that keep them from reaching their potential.

At its core, seeking purpose assumes a foundation of stability, both financially and mentally. Imagine, for a moment, someone juggling two low-wage jobs just to make ends meet, or a single parent who has to prioritize food, shelter, and childcare. For them, the idea of "finding your purpose" might not only seem irrelevant— it can feel like a cruel joke. When survival is the focus of your every day, any talk of purpose can ring hollow, unachievable, and even exhausting.

I know this feeling all too well. I have been in survival mode. I've had to work long hours just to make ends meet, often without benefits or security. When your life is defined by the constant need to manage the day-to-day, purpose seems like a distant, unattainable goal. I remember the long hours I spent commuting between jobs, the emotional toll of job instability, the worries that weighed me down: bills, car repairs, the struggle to support my family. There was little room left in my mind even to consider "purpose," let alone pursue it.

During these times, clarity of mind becomes invaluable—yet it is a resource that not everyone has access to. In my experience, time and mental space to reflect and explore what might fulfill me or give my life meaning were a luxury often out of reach. These things are not usually valued in the everyday grind of survival. To even *imagine* having the luxury of self-actualization was an impossible dream when I was consumed by constant survival.

This is where purpose-seeking becomes a privilege. People who are fortunate enough to have their basic needs met, who are not preoccupied with how they will feed their children or pay rent next month, are the ones who have the luxury to pause, reflect, and search for purpose. They have the time and mental energy to explore what truly fulfills them, free from the day-to-day anxieties that many of us face. For them, purpose is something to be lived and celebrated, not chased after when survival is uncertain.

Purpose rhetoric often ignores these disparities. It paints a picture of purpose as something universally accessible—something everyone can attain if they just look or work hard enough. This narrative doesn't acknowledge the structural inequalities that make it incredibly difficult for many to *consider* such an ideal. It creates a false equivalence, assuming that everyone starts on the same footing, and it disregards the barriers created by race, gender, economic status, and other intersecting factors.

For instance, marginalized communities face compounded barriers: discrimination in education and employment, limited access to healthcare, and often, a lack of physical safety. When survival is a daily battle, "finding your purpose" becomes almost irrelevant. For these individuals, purpose is not about fulfillment or passion but survival. It's about resilience and the determination to persevere despite overwhelming odds.

When we think about who often gets to display their purpose-driven life publicly, it is typically those in positions of power, influence, or financial security. The entrepreneurs, the celebrities, the influencers—those with the means to build a personal brand around their "passion." These are the individuals whose lives are not weighed down by the barriers that others face. They are not trapped in survival mode, scrambling to make ends meet. Their journeys are often polished, framed as aspirational models of success. And yet, their visibility in the purpose-driven discourse only widens the gap between them and those whose stories remain untold.

Social media amplifies this divide. On these platforms, images of people living out their purpose—often by working meaningful jobs, traveling, or investing in personal growth—dominate the conversation. These people live lives of luxury and freedom, and the implicit message is clear: if you're not living this way, you're missing out. Worse, until you reach your "purpose," you won't experience these types of opportunities. Whether intentional or not, this idea places blame on those stuck in survival mode, ignoring the structural forces that make such freedoms accessible only to some.

This also highlights another problem with the purpose narrative: it subtly implies that those not actively seeking a "higher" purpose are somehow lacking. They are dismissed as unambitious, as if their lives are meaningless or less valuable. Yet, for many people, the absence of purpose is not a choice—it's the result of external circumstances far beyond their control. Survival mode doesn't leave much room for lofty existential goals; it demands focus on the immediate.

This exclusionary view reinforces the idea that there is only one valid way to live—a fulfilling life centers on purpose. But this overlooks the rich diversity of human experience. For some, fulfillment may come from simply maintaining stability, supporting family, or navigating daily challenges with resilience. These are powerful, meaningful ways to live, but they don't always fit into the narrow framework of "purpose-seeking" that society tells us is the only path to fulfillment.

CHAPTER 4

PURPOSE PARALYSIS

ave you ever heard of "analysis paralysis"? It's when too many options overwhelm you to the point of inaction. Purpose paralysis is a close cousin. It's when the constant search for your "purpose" keeps you frozen, unable to live fully in the present or make decisions, all because you're constantly questioning whether each choice aligns with a grand, life-defining mission.

Think about it—when it's time to make a decision, we all naturally weigh the options. We assess what outcome we want and choose the path that we think will lead us there. For some, this process is tangled up in a deeper question: *Will this choice lead me to my ultimate purpose?* If you've ever hesitated to make a decision, or worse, backed out altogether, because you feared it might not align with your "bigger mission," you know exactly what I mean.

This mindset can create a trap, where each decision feels like it's more than just a decision—it's a choice that could either bring you closer to your life's purpose or push you further away. But here's the thing: that pressure, that weight of needing every choice to be "right," is exactly what leads to purpose paralysis.

Now, let's pause for a moment. Think about a time you've faced a decision—big or small—and felt paralyzed by the fear of making the wrong one. The fear of "getting it wrong" is all too common. But what if I told you that the fear of making the wrong choice isn't about failing at life, but rather about being overly fixated on the idea that one misstep will derail your entire journey?

Learn to Trust Your Intuition Again

There isn't a single "right" way to go most of the time. Life isn't about finding the one true path and following it unthinkingly; it's about the journey itself—the experiences you have, the lessons you learn, and the people you meet along the way. Every choice doesn't have to be part of some greater, predetermined plan. Sometimes, simply making a choice—no matter how small—allows you to experience life more authentically and more fulfilling.

This is where choosing "just because it feels right" comes in. What if, instead of placing every decision under the microscope of your grand life's purpose, you allowed yourself to simply *live* in the moment? Imagine making a choice because it feels aligned with who you are *right now*—not because it fits some idea of who you think you should become or where you think you should be heading.

Freedom lies in letting go of purpose and choosing what feels right without attaching significance. Ironically, removing pressure makes decisions easier, lighter, and more enjoyable. You liberate yourself from purpose's chains and embrace a more relaxed, fulfilling life.

You see, purpose paralysis doesn't just prevent us from acting; it steals our ability to be fully present. When we're always focused on the "right" decision, we miss the beauty of simply *being*. It's like we're standing at the crossroads of life, obsessing over which path to take, when in reality, every path leads to some form of growth, some form of experience.

Life Isn't a Straight Line

Purpose paralysis often results from the belief that life must follow a linear, upward trajectory. We imagine a ladder we must climb, with each step representing progress toward our greater purpose. However, life isn't a ladder—it's more like a loop. At times, we circle back to things we thought we had moved on from. Progress isn't always about climbing higher; it can also mean returning to something familiar with a new understanding.

Let go of linear thinking. Instead of seeing life as a ladder you must climb, imagine it as a series of loops or cycles. Maybe you'll revisit old interests, make the same decision twice, or return to a place you thought you had outgrown. Trust that these "loops" are still progress—they allow you to integrate and grow in ways that a straight path doesn't.

For much of my adult life, I was consumed by the fear of making the wrong choice. I constantly searched for purpose, convinced that every decision had to fit into some grand narrative. For years, I second-guessed every move, believing that one misstep would destroy my chance at living a meaningful life.

You Don't Have to Justify Your Existence

But it wasn't until I started letting go of that need for perfection, that need for everything to have a higher meaning, that I finally felt free. I realized that it was okay not to have everything figured out. Sometimes, just *living* in the moment—making decisions because they felt right for me—was enough.

I spent so much time fearing I was off track, I forgot that life wasn't meant to be a perfectly planned journey. Instead, it's a collection of moments, choices, and experiences. And the more I embraced that idea, the more at peace I became with the path I was on.

Purpose doesn't have to be the lens through which we view every decision. Sometimes, it's enough just to live and trust that the pieces will fall into place. You don't have to have everything figured out right now. You are enough, just as you are, and every choice you make is an opportunity to discover more about who you are—and who you're becoming.

CHAPTER 5

PERMISSION TO SIMPLY LIVE

For a long time, I believed that purpose had to be a grand, singular concept. I thought I needed to discover that one significant thing that defined me and provided a sense of meaning. The pressure to determine it made me feel as though I was perpetually chasing something just beyond my grasp, as if my entire life hinged on uncovering my purpose. However, I've come to realize that purpose isn't just one major idea. Instead, it often exists in fragments, embedded within the small moments we encounter daily, the relationships we foster with others, and the simple acts of kindness we offer and receive.

Purpose doesn't have to be a force that dictates every choice. Sometimes, purpose is about living well finding meaning in the small things, the moments that feel right, and letting them shape who we are. It can be found in a conversation with a friend, the joy of doing something you love, or simply being present in the here and now. Life is full of moments, and each of those moments, no matter how small, can contribute to a purposeful life if we stop searching for purpose in some grand, distant future.

And here's the real freedom: it's okay not to have a **singular** purpose and to just exist without feeling like every action needs to be part of some larger mission or grand scheme. When we stop overthinking it and stop seeing every choice as a test of our purpose, we can start living and being happy in the now.

I want to share something important: living in the moment, embracing daily joys and challenges without the constant pressure of aligning everything with some grand idea of purpose, is a form of fulfillment. Just being is enough, in case nobody ever told you. You are here, you are exactly where you should be.

We've been sold this idea that purpose is about achieving something huge, but the truth is, if you need to feel a sense of purpose, I want you to know that I can simply be about being present; it doesn't need to be grand or some profound revelation. It's about finding contentment in the small, everyday moments and knowing you're enough just as you are, here and now. You don't have to have all the answers to live a meaningful life—you just need to give yourself the freedom to live it without the weight of perfection or grand expectations.

An Old Lesson to Unlearn

From a young age, we're taught our purpose, whenever we discover it, defines us, gives our life meaning, and serves as a guidepost for every decision we make. Society reinforces this idea with countless stories of people who seemed to know exactly what they were 'meant' to do, as if their purpose was waiting for them all along, clear and unwavering.

This idea, while inspiring to some, can feel suffocating to others. After all, what happens if you never find that one big thing? Or worse, what if the thing you thought was your purpose doesn't feel fulfilling anymore? Does this mean you will never be successful, happy, or have a life worth living?

Purpose doesn't need to be a singular, unyielding mission; that is a myth. You can live a meaningful life without searching for "the one big thing." For years, I felt restricted by this belief, as if each choice had to align with a single purpose, like walking a tightrope, afraid to stray from the expected path.

But what if purpose could be more flexible? What if it consisted of small acts, curiosities, and connections that evolve as we grow? This understanding—that I didn't require a singular purpose to have a meaningful life—brought me immense relief. I could finally explore, make mistakes, and appreciate things I had previously overlooked, without having to link them to a larger purpose.

A Journey of Realization

Like many, I used to think that finding my purpose hinged on picking the "right" career. For a long time, I believed nursing would allow me to make a difference and be fulfilled. However, everything changed in an instant. During a class, we encountered a cadaver, and the shock and paralysis hit me so profoundly that I couldn't recover for weeks. Suddenly, nursing felt off the table, leaving me to ponder, "If I can't be a nurse, then what is my purpose?"

After regrouping, I entered public health—a field that still allowed me to help people without the demands of patient care. I earned a bachelor's and a master's degree, built a career, and gained experience. On the surface, I felt accomplished, but something was missing. I didn't feel the fulfillment I'd been chasing.

That's when my partner shared his dream of starting a real estate investment business. At first, I saw it as something small, a side project, but as we both invested more time and energy into it, I began feeling a growing tension. My partner was fully committed, often saying that real estate was his purpose—the reason he woke up excited each day. Every new property we bought seemed to ignite his passion. He embraced every challenge with a smile, always talking about how privileged he felt to live his purpose, no matter how tough things got.

I'll be honest: I felt deeply jealous when he said that. I had never really understood what "green with envy" meant until those moments. I envied his clarity and his certainty about his purpose. While I was still searching, he seemed to have it all figured out. So, I doubled down on my work in public health, hoping that by giving more of myself to it, it would finally feel like my own "big purpose." But it didn't. Real estate was never my thing, and I wasn't handling the pressure like he was. Each time we acquired a new property, I felt nauseous, overwhelmed by the stress and obstacles that came with it.

It wasn't the real estate that left me feeling lost; rather, my yearning for a singular, defining purpose triggered my spiraling thoughts. Despite my efforts to push forward, I couldn't shake off the sense that I wasn't in the right place. Lacking my partner's unwavering confidence made me feel like I was falling behind.

The Turning Point

Working part-time on the business, I started to resent it. Each time the company grew, my frustration deepened. It seemed like we were building his dream and purpose, and I didn't know where I fit. I began to wonder: What about me? Where was my purpose in all this?

I never admitted this to my partner, but he sensed it. After all, we've been together long enough that he knows me well, probably more than I'd like to admit. He'll finally read about it here, in these pages.

I had to face the uncomfortable truth: I was placing too much pressure on the idea that I had to choose between my career and the business. The struggle wasn't about one path being right or wrong—it was about the season I was in. Building the business didn't have to represent some grand purpose or the end of my public health career. It wasn't a matter of finding "the one thing." It was simply another experience I could explore.

Once I stopped chasing deeper, life-defining meaning, I started to be fully present in my work. Instead of getting caught up in whether it was my "purpose" or not, I embraced the day-to-day challenges, focused on learning, and took initiative where I could. To my surprise, the business began to thrive in ways I hadn't even imagined—because I was finally in it, not as a means to prove something, but as a step in my journey.

A New Perspective on Purpose

That shift in mindset—letting go of the search for ultimate purpose was freeing. It helped me embrace the present, focus on what I could control, and savor the journey instead of fixating on an elusive end goal. I discovered a deep happiness and fulfillment I hadn't anticipated. Before I realized it, the business reached a major milestone, surpassing a million in revenue—something unimaginable when we began this venture. It showed the power of being present and trusting the process.

I might have missed this entirely if I'd remained fixated on finding a singular purpose. Sometimes, purpose isn't one big thing we search for but a collection of small, meaningful actions that accumulate over time. Letting go of rigid expectations allowed me to discover fulfillment in the present.

So, if you feel lost or questioning your path, know that it's okay to simply live, take each step as it comes, and allow joy, fulfillment, and certainty to evolve naturally. If you seek a purpose, please know that it doesn't have to be fixed or singular—it can shift and adapt, just like we do as humans.

I want to extend a challenge: if you ever start feeling lost, anxious, or uncertain in your journey through life, I want you to stop, look around, and just be for a second. Clear your mind, breathe slowly, and exist uninterrupted for about 30 minutes if you can. Breathe deeply and feel the air filling your lungs. Feel the beat of your heart.

That's you, simply being. And it's beautiful. And it's enough. You can give yourself permission to just live.

CHAPTER 6

PURPOSE VS. PASSION

Is There Really a Difference?

In a world urging us to "find our purpose," it's easy to confuse purpose with passion. Though similar, they lead to different life paths. Purpose indicates an overarching mission or meaning, driving us toward something larger than ourselves. Conversely, passion involves intense enthusiasm for something specific, often focused on the present rather than a lifelong goal. According to Merriam-Webster, *passion* is "a strong feeling of enthusiasm or excitement for something or about doing something." This intensity is immediate and personal, motivating us to engage deeply with what we love. Unlike purpose, which feels heavy and enduring, passion is lighter, evolving, and often brings joy to our pursuits.

When we try to equate purpose and passion, we can find ourselves in a state of exhaustion, feeling trapped by our own expectations. For example, let's say you have a deep passion for photography. You love capturing moments and sharing them with friends, but then you decide to turn it into a full-time career because you feel pressure to elevate it to something significant that leads to discovering your "purpose." Suddenly, the passion becomes a burden: you have deadlines, clients, and expectations to meet. What was once a source of joy and an escape from the demanding toil of life has now turned into a source of stress and, over time, even resentment.

I want to clarify that this doesn't mean purpose-driven careers aren't valuable; they certainly are. But it's important to recognize that turning every passion into a life mission or overarching purpose might strip it of the very enjoyment and freedom it once offered. In many cases, people benefit from keeping passions as something flexible, allowing them to shift and change with time.

Complementary, But Not the Same

The distinction between purpose and passion is not new, and many successful figures have explored it in their own journeys. Marie Forleo, in her book *Everything is Figureoutable*, argues against the pressure to find a single purpose, suggesting instead that people follow multiple passions and explore varied interests to create a fulfilling life. She emphasizes that purpose and passion are separate entities that can both contribute to our sense of satisfaction.

Oprah Winfrey has also spoken extensively about the importance of passion and purpose, often distinguishing between the two in her own life. While she has built a career rooted in purpose, she credits passion as the force that initially drew her into media and kept her deeply engaged along the way.

Mark Manson, author of *The Subtle Art of Not Giving a F*ck*, offers a grounded perspective on purpose and passion. He suggests that while purpose can give structure to our lives, it's important not to rely too heavily on it, as it may not always lead to happiness. In Manson's view, passion brings immediacy and motivation, while purpose provides direction. The two work best together when viewed as complementary rather than identical.

Understanding the difference between purpose and passion helps us adopt a lighter approach to life. By easing the pressure to find a single, all-consuming purpose, we welcome various interests and experiences that can evolve. This is crucial as people and their interests change over time—what ignited our passion in our twenties may look different in our thirties or forties. A life filled with multiple passions—without needing to tie them to a grand purpose—provides freedom and adaptability.

Consider those who explore various interests and have careers that aren't purpose-driven but provide stability, while they pursue their passions on the side. Their lives are no less fulfilling—in fact, they're often more well-rounded and content than if they felt pressured to chase "one true calling." For them, balancing a stable career and engaging passions brings a unique sense of fulfillment that might be lost if they combined the two.

Where Purpose Guides, Passion Explores

I know what you are thinking: "*Don't purpose and passion usually align?*" My opinion is that while they *can*, they **don't** have to. Passion and purpose don't need to be intertwined to create a meaningful life. Separating them can allow for a sense of freedom and balance that prevents burnout, which frequently happens when we try to turn every passion into a purpose.

Knowing the difference between passion and purpose also prevents us from feeling like failures if our passions don't align with a greater mission. It frees us to navigate life flexibly and enjoy what we love without the weight of making it something monumental. In fact, this separation allows us to savor our passions fully and pursue purpose in ways that enrich rather than overwhelm. Embracing this distinction can be liberating, allowing us to construct a meaningful life on our own terms.

As you reflect on your life, think about the things that truly light you up. Give yourself permission to pursue passion without feeling obligated to turn it into purpose.

Invitation for Ongoing Reflection

As you explore your passions and reflect on the differences and benefits of enjoying moments in life without a connection to a greater mission, remember that the two don't have to be one and the same. Allow yourself to:

- *Follow your passions just because they bring you joy,* not because they have to contribute to a larger purpose or make you "successful" in the eyes of others.
- *Engage in activities that excite you simply for the sake of the experience,* whether or not they lead to anything permanent or extraordinary. Sometimes, an activity's value lies solely in the joy it brings in the moment.
- *Allow your passions to evolve and change over time,* without feeling like you're abandoning them. It's okay to grow out of specific interests and find new ones; your worth doesn't depend on sticking to one thing forever.

- *Reflect on past passions that you let go of,* and ask yourself what they taught you. Sometimes, a passion's impact on your life is not in its continuation, but in the lessons or experiences you gain.
- *Notice the sense of freedom that comes with releasing the need to "make everything count."* When you allow yourself to simply *be* in the moment with your passions, life becomes richer and less stressful.

Reflecting on these ideas enables you to live freely, appreciating your passions in the present without tying them to a bigger plan. This approach can lead to a fulfilling, balanced life that doesn't feel like a race to a specific endpoint.

CHAPTER 7

RETHINKING DECISIONS

Why Purpose Doesn't Matter as Much as You Think

For years, I believed every decision had to serve a greater purpose. I thought the "right" decision was the one that perfectly aligned with some predetermined mission—a deeper calling that was supposed to guide every step I took. I clung to this idea because it gave me a sense of control and belief that everything would fall into place if I found and stayed on the right path. But here's the problem with that mindset: **chasing the illusion of purpose made me feel trapped.** It turned every choice into a heavy, almost unbearable burden.

This pressure made even small decisions feel monumental. Where to live, what job to take, what opportunities to pursue—each choice felt like a test I couldn't afford to fail. It left me paralyzed, constantly second-guessing myself and questioning whether I was moving closer to or further from this mythical "higher purpose."

But then I started asking myself different questions: *What if the only wrong choice is not making one at all?* What if waiting for a perfect alignment—or some divine sign—was just another way of keeping myself stuck? What if passivity is a choice that we make everyday? These questions shifted my perspective in ways I never expected.

The obsession with purpose makes us believe decisions fall into one of two categories: *right* or *wrong*. This binary thinking creates unnecessary pressure, as if every step must be perfectly aligned with some imagined higher calling to be valid.

But here's the truth: **most decisions aren't that black and white.** What makes a decision "right" or "wrong" is often just a matter of perspective—and time. Sometimes, the "wrong" choices lead to the best lessons, and the "right" ones leave us feeling empty.

Instead of asking, "Does this decision align with my purpose?" I started asking, "Does this decision feel *good enough for* right now?" And everything changed. Most of life's choices don't need to be perfect or calculated; they just need to move us forward.

A Personal Story: When "Good Enough" Was Exactly What I Needed

Let me take you back to a time when everything felt like it was falling apart. A year after graduating, I struggled to find a job in my field. Like many new graduates, I had big dreams—reality had other plans. I rented an apartment with a friend, scraping by with no savings, maxed-out credit cards, and a negative balance. My car was on its last legs, barely getting me from point A to point B.

Then came the curveball. My roommate decided to move out, leaving me with less than thirty days to figure out my next steps. I was not financially prepared for this upheaval. I remember calling my mom in tears, feeling gutted. She told me to pray and have faith that something would come through. Skeptical but desperate, I did just that.

A week later, my uncle Earl called unexpectedly. He was moving to his large house in Georgia and suggested I rent a room. It wasn't my ideal solution—it felt like a step backward, not forward. But it was my only option. So, I packed my things and moved in, planning to stay just long enough to get back on my feet.

Georgia wasn't an easy landing. I struggled to find a job and drove for Uber and Lyft just to make ends meet. It was exhausting, humbling work. Meanwhile, I had just started my graduate school courses online, juggling the weight of academic expectations with the stress of unemployment. I remember lying awake at night, frustrated and questioning how my life had veered so far off course.

Eventually, I started a job at a health insurance call center. It wasn't glamorous, and it certainly wasn't the kind of position I had envisioned for myself with a college degree. Walking into that office on my first day, I felt crushed, as though I'd failed some unspoken promise to myself. But as much as I hated being there, I needed the paycheck.

After about a month, something unexpected happened. During one of my breaks, I spoke with an older woman who worked there. She shared her own career journey and casually suggested I look into temporary contract roles with the health department. It was a fleeting comment, but it planted a seed. That evening, I went home and searched online. Sure enough, I found a temporary position listed with the Georgia Department of Public Health as a Disease Intervention Specialist. Without hesitation, I applied.

To my surprise, I got the job. It wasn't just a paycheck—it was a foot in the door to a career path in my field. That call center job, which I had once resented so deeply, had been the steppingstone I didn't realize I needed.

Looking back, I can see how that series of events taught me an invaluable lesson: sometimes, "good enough" is all you need in the moment. At the time, I only saw the disappointment of not being where I thought I should be. But taking that job, making that move, and simply focusing on what I needed at the time eventually created opportunities I couldn't have planned for.

Why Perfect Alignment is a Myth

This experience made me realize one of the most pervasive myths about purpose: the idea of "perfect alignment." We're often told that every decision must fit neatly into some overarching mission, building toward a specific, meaningful destination. But this belief creates an impossible standard.

Life is messy, unpredictable, and rarely unfolds according to a master plan. Sometimes, the best choices are the ones that seem completely disconnected from any grand idea of purpose. They're the decisions we make simply because they feel right at the time, or because they're "good enough" for the moment. Ironically, these choices often lead us to the most valuable experiences, unexpected lessons, and opportunities we never could have planned for.

Decisions Don't Define You—Action Does

The real problem isn't making the wrong decision; it's letting fear or overthinking stop you from making any decision at all. Living a meaningful life has less to do with purpose and more with action. It's about showing up, making choices, and allowing yourself to move forward—even if those choices don't come with a deep sense of alignment or certainty.

We free ourselves when we let go of the need for every decision to serve a higher purpose. We allow ourselves to live, explore, and grow without the limits of chasing some elusive, perfect idea of purpose. And in the end, it's this freedom, not the pursuit of alignment, that makes life truly meaningful.

Reflection and Practical Advice

As you think about your own life, ask yourself:

- How many decisions have you avoided because you feared they didn't align with some bigger plan or support a personal identity?
- What choices could you make today if you let go of the need for perfection or purpose?

Keep the following in mind as you make decisions for yourself:

- Stop waiting for the "perfect" choice. The perfect decision doesn't exist. Waiting for it will only keep you stuck.
- Focus on what feels right for now. A good enough choice is still progress, and progress is what matters.
- Trust the process. Even the smallest decisions carry lessons and opportunities. You don't need a higher purpose to validate them.
- Redefine success. Success isn't about alignment with a grand plan. It's about growth, exploration, and the courage to try something new.

By embracing imperfection and rejecting the pressure of purpose, you allow yourself to move forward in ways you never thought possible.

CHAPTER 8

PURPOSE DOESN'T OWN YOU

Thriving Without a Plan

For most of my life, I believed in the illusion that every decision had to have a clear, meaningful purpose behind it. I convinced myself that every move I made needed to be part of some bigger plan, some greater mission. And if it didn't fit into that grand vision, I saw it as a failure or a waste of time. The pressure to figure everything out was overwhelming, but it felt like the only way to make my life count.

But here's the thing: the more I clung to that idea, the more trapped I became. I kept waiting for clarity, for the perfect opportunity to come along, for that one big breakthrough that would make everything make sense. I was constantly scanning the horizon, hoping for a sign. Yet, as much as I looked for it, that moment never came.

Then, something shifted—slowly, almost imperceptibly. It wasn't one big, earth-shattering revelation. It was more of a gradual unraveling. I realized I wasn't missing the "perfect" path—I was holding myself back by waiting for it to appear. I had spent so much time fixated on the idea of purpose that I hadn't noticed how much life was happening around me, without a map or a script.

Toni Morrison once said, "You are your best thing." This statement resonates deeply in a world that constantly tells us to strive for perfection, have a clear plan, and meet external expectations. It reminds us that our true strength and beauty lie in embracing who we are, imperfections and all. When we stop chasing an idealized version of ourselves or a meticulously planned future, we begin to tap into the richness of our authentic selves.

The truth was, the more I embraced uncertainty and gave up the need for a concrete plan, the more I started moving forward, even without knowing exactly where I was going. This was the hardest part to admit to myself— that I didn't have to have everything figured out to move. The more I tried to plan my life down to the finest detail, the more I realized that life, by its very nature, doesn't follow a neat script. No amount of planning could prevent the unexpected twists and turns.

The Illusion of Control

Purpose and planning sound comforting—they provide a sense of safety. However, sometimes, the pursuit of these elements only slows us down. It creates a false sense of control, a belief that if we meticulously map everything out in advance, we'll somehow become immune to the chaos that life inevitably brings. But what if that chaos is precisely where the magic happens?

I've had moments when I didn't know if I was making the right decision. I looked at the uncertainty ahead and felt both fear and exhilaration. Some of my defining moments—whether in my personal life, career, or even my decisions—came from stepping into the unknown. It was never easy, but those moments shaped me the most. They were the times when I had no clear idea what the outcome would be, but I decided to keep going anyway.

I was terrified the first time I took a risk and moved forward without a clear destination. It felt like a leap into an abyss, yet I was drawn to the unknown. In that leap, I found strength, resilience, and a deeper understanding of what truly mattered to me. The times when I embraced uncertainty instead of trying to control it were the moments when my world expanded in ways I had never imagined.

Over time, I realized that thriving without a plan isn't about being reckless or aimless. It's about learning to trust the process, even when the destination isn't clear. It's about leaning into the discomfort of not knowing and accepting that not everything needs to have a defined purpose to be valuable. The beauty of not having a rigid road map is that you open yourself up to possibilities you never would have considered if you were following a "perfect" plan. You begin to see opportunities in unexpected places, and doors open that you didn't even know existed.

Instead of pushing against the current, you start to flow with it.

Letting go when every fiber of your being screams to hold on feels like standing on a cliff edge, the wind howling, urging you to jump while your mind races with reasons to stay. The ground beneath you is solid and familiar, but cracks have appeared. The cliff isn't as safe as it once seemed, yet stepping off into the unknown is paralyzing.

Fear grips you, whispering that the fall could destroy you. What if there's no net? What if the leap leads to pain, failure, or regret? Doubt creeps in, weaving stories in your mind: What if there's nothing worth finding? What if all of this—the struggle, the risk—is for nothing?

And so, you cling tighter. To the plan. To the illusion of control. To the version of life you've convinced yourself is "safe." But control is a fickle friend. It gives an illusion of order, the belief that we can bend life's unpredictable currents. We're conditioned to believe that control equals safety, that having a plan shields us from chaos. Society tells us that if we just work hard and plan meticulously, we can avoid uncertainty.

Flexibility Is Strength

But what happens when life doesn't cooperate? When plans fall apart, or worse, never come together? What about when the very thing you're clinging to begins to crumble in your hands, leaving you grasping at air?

In these moments, we face the greatest test—not of our strength, but of our willingness to release. Releasing control doesn't mean the fear vanishes. The fear will always be there, standing beside you at the cliff's edge, whispering its warnings. But fear doesn't have to own you.

Letting go is not an act of weakness—it is an act of courage. It's stepping off the edge with nothing but faith that the air will carry you, that the fall will transform you, and that the landing, wherever it may be, will teach you what you need to know.

Here's a truth that society often overlooks: freedom lies in the fall. The thrill of venturing into the unknown is the upside of fear. It's the excitement of understanding that control was never the objective. Freedom isn't about possessing all the answers or guaranteeing that every step is pre-planned; it's about having faith that you will discover the answers along the way.

When you stop clinging and begin trusting, the cliff transforms. The wind that once felt like a threat becomes a force that carries you forward. The emptiness you feared becomes a space for infinite possibilities. And the ground you thought was your foundation reveals itself for what it truly was: a starting point, not a destination.

So, what if the fall isn't the end but the beginning? What if releasing control isn't about losing everything but discovering something greater—your resilience, courage, and ability to thrive in the unknown?

Letting go is never easy. It will stretch you, unmake you, and remake you. But in the process, it will free you.

Letting go of a meticulously planned life doesn't mean you abandon direction. It means accepting that the most important step is sometimes the one you take without knowing where it leads. The path reveals itself as you walk it. You learn to trust your intuition and that it's okay not to have all the answers. The unknown becomes less scary and more exciting.

Purpose doesn't own you. When you let go of the need to have everything figured out, you unlock the freedom to live more fully, authentically, and with greater possibilities than you could ever have planned. The uncertainty isn't something to fear—it's an invitation to step into the unknown, make mistakes, learn, grow, and ultimately, thrive.

PRACTICAL ADVICE: EMBRACE THE UNKNOWN

- **Trust yourself:** Let go of the need for certainty and make decisions that feel good in the moment. Trust that your choices now will lead you somewhere important, even if it's not immediately obvious.
- **Take calculated risks:** Living without a clear plan doesn't mean living recklessly. It's about evaluating the risks, but not letting fear or the absence of a perfect path keep you from moving forward.
- **Find freedom in ambiguity:** The unknown isn't something to fear—it's something to embrace. Not knowing what's next is often where the greatest opportunities lie.
- **Focus on action, not alignment:** It's not about making decisions that align perfectly with some grand vision. It's about making decisions and moving forward. Action creates momentum, and momentum leads to new possibilities.

A Challenge for the Week: Letting Go of the Plan

This week, I challenge you to actively release your grip on a plan or an aspect of your life that you've been tightly controlling. It could be a decision that feels impossible to make, a project you've been meticulously planning, or a point you need to reach before taking action.

IDENTIFY THE PLAN

- Take a moment to pinpoint the plan, goal, or idea you've been clinging to. Write it down. Why have you been holding onto it so tightly? What fears or anxieties are tied to not having everything figured out? Acknowledge these feelings without judgment—they're part of being human.

RELEASE CONTROL

- This week, challenge yourself to take one step toward releasing that control. It doesn't mean you have to abandon your plan entirely, but it does mean allowing yourself to move forward in a new way. Maybe you stop overthinking, let go of some perfectionist tendencies, or take action with little to no preparation.

DO SOMETHING UNPLANNED

- As part of this challenge, say "yes" to an opportunity or decision you wouldn't normally consider because it doesn't fit into your current plan. This might mean attending a networking event you'd typically avoid, trying a new hobby, saying "yes" to an invitation that doesn't fit your schedule, or taking a break when you feel like you "should" be working. The goal is to open yourself to something spontaneous and uncharted.

STEP INTO DISCOMFORT

- Embrace the discomfort of uncertainty. Let yourself feel the unease of not knowing what comes next. Pay attention to the discomfort and reflect on it. What does it teach you about yourself? Do you feel liberated or anxious? Notice the tension between your desire for control and the freedom of letting go.

TRUST THE PROCESS

- As you engage in this challenge, remember that it's not about a perfect outcome but the process itself. Trust that moving forward without a rigid plan opens doors to new possibilities you may not have known existed. Stay open to whatever unfolds, knowing that a specific path does not define you.

REFLECT AND JOURNAL

At the end of the week, come back to these reflections. Take time to journal about your experience:

- How did it feel to move forward without a plan?
- What was the hardest part about letting go of control?
- Did anything surprising happen when you released your grip on the plan?

- Did you learn anything new about yourself or the situation you were holding onto?
- Did this experience shift how you view uncertainty and control in your life?

ACTION BEYOND THE WEEK

After completing the challenge, consider integrating the lessons learned into your daily life. What would it look like to trust the process more often? Can you identify more opportunities where releasing control can lead to personal growth or unexpected outcomes?

CHAPTER 9

TRUSTING THE JOURNEY, NOT THE PLAN

In this book, I've invite you to question the conventional wisdom that our lives require a singular purpose. I encourage you to reconsider whether purpose truly unlocks all of life's answers. We've been led to believe that finding purpose brings clarity, meaning, and success, but what if that's not the answer we need?

What if thriving isn't about discovering one purpose or ensuring every decision is part of some grand plan? What if letting go of the need for purpose entirely is the key to truly living?

Life doesn't follow a script. The more I clung to the idea that there was one right path to follow, the more frustrated and stuck I felt. I waited for clarity, the perfect opportunity, and that big breakthrough to tie it all together. But it never came. What did come, though, was the realization that I didn't need all the answers to keep moving forward. I didn't need a detailed blueprint for every step.

And that's where I found my freedom. By letting go of the need for a clear plan, I gave myself the space to just live, take chances, make mistakes, and follow unexpected paths. The more I leaned into the uncertainty, the more I thrived.

I want you to consider this: the moments that truly shape us are often the ones we didn't plan for. Think about all the times in your life when things didn't go as expected. In the moment, those missteps may have seemed like failures, but in hindsight, they were the moments that pushed you to grow. You learned, adapted, and ended up somewhere you never could have anticipated—but it worked out. Why? Because life unfolded in its own beautiful, unpredictable way. You didn't need to control it; you just needed to trust it.

No Two Journeys Are the Same

Trusting the journey looks different for everyone. For someone dealing with grief or the loss of a loved one, trusting the journey might mean giving yourself permission to feel the full weight of your emotions without rushing to "get over it." Healing isn't linear, and it doesn't arrive on a schedule. Trusting the journey in this context is about recognizing that even in the depths of loss, there is space for eventual peace and clarity. It's about allowing the process to unfold, even when it feels unbearable, and believing that your pain will someday transform into strength and a deeper understanding of love.

Going through a separation or divorce can feel like stepping into a void where everything familiar has been stripped away. Here, the journey is about embracing the uncertainty of this in-between space, even when it feels daunting. This period of discomfort isn't the end; it's the beginning of a new chapter. Trusting the journey means believing that this upheaval is clearing the way for a more aligned and fulfilling life, even if you can't fully imagine it yet.

For someone facing a particularly challenging period in their life, trusting the journey means reframing struggles as part of a larger story. It may not feel meaningful or purposeful now, but every hurdle you overcome shapes your resilience and strength. Even when progress feels slow or invisible, each small step forward builds momentum. Trusting the journey here is not about minimizing your challenges but about honoring them as critical parts of your growth.

For the career-driven individual, trusting the journey might mean accepting an unexpected role or opportunity, even if it doesn't seem like the perfect fit. It's about seeing value in the experience itself rather than being fixated on a specific end goal. Trusting the journey allows you to explore, adapt, and discover new paths that might be even more fulfilling than you originally planned.

For the perfectionist, trusting the journey means loosening the grip on needing everything, embracing the messiness of progress, and understanding that forward movement, however imperfect, is what truly matters. Trusting the journey here means choosing to start, even when the outcome isn't guaranteed.

For someone facing deep uncertainty, trusting the journey is about finding the courage to take one step at a time, even without a clear view of what's ahead. It's believing that clarity often comes in motion, not in waiting. It's a reminder that you don't need all the answers to keep moving forward.

In these situations, trusting the journey is an active, intentional choice. It's leaning into discomfort, embracing the unknown, and allowing life to surprise you. It's not easy, but it's where growth, healing, and transformation happen.

Letting Go of Perfection

Your life doesn't have to be a perfect, planned-out journey. Striving for that often holds you back. The desire for perfection and certainty can paralyze you. It can stop you from stepping out, exploring, or creating something new. It keeps you trapped in a cycle of second-guessing and waiting for the "perfect" moment that will never come.

So, what if you let life surprise you instead of chasing after purpose? What if you trusted the journey instead of obsessing over the destination? What if you allowed the chaos, the unpredictability, the messiness of life to be a part of your story—and found joy in it?

I'm inviting you to do just that. Let go of the need for a concrete plan. Embrace the discomfort of not knowing exactly what comes next. Let go of the idea that your life needs to fit into a perfect, predictable mold. Because, in that space—the unknown, the messy, the unplanned—is where actual growth happens.

Ultimately, succeeding without a plan doesn't equate to recklessness; it involves having faith in the process. It allows you to progress without the burden of knowing your exact destination. By embracing uncertainty with confidence, you invite new possibilities and opportunities you could never have envisioned before.

This book is your invitation to embrace the uncertainty of life. Trust that even when you don't have all the answers, you can still take meaningful steps. You don't need a perfect road map to create a fulfilling life. You just need the courage to keep moving, even when the path isn't clear.

A Final Thought

As you reach the end of this book, you might notice something unconventional. There's no Chapter 10.

This isn't a mistake nor a sign that I ran out of things to say. Ending at Chapter 9 is intentional. It reflects everything I've shared with you in these pages. Life doesn't need a neatly wrapped-up conclusion. It doesn't need to end on an even number or a perfectly packaged final thought. It's an ongoing process that doesn't have to be perfectly structured or easily understood.

By ending here, I'm leaving you with something real. Life continues, and so does your journey. There's no definitive conclusion to reach, no final destination to arrive at. This is how I want this book to leave you— open-ended, free from the pressure to figure everything out, and ready to embrace whatever comes next.

Life is messy. It's unpredictable. And that's what makes it so beautiful.

The world often tells us we're not truly living until we've found our purpose, until everything feels aligned. But here's the reality: you are living, and that's enough. So, when you feel cornered by the idea that you're not 'there' yet, just pause and remember you're already "here."

And that's enough.

ACKNOWLEDGMENTS

First and foremost, I want to thank my husband, Demarcus Dubose, whose entrepreneurial spirit and steadfast support were foundational to this book's development. His encouragement throughout my writing journey pushed me to persevere, complete this project, and reminded me that every step no matter how small is important.

I am deeply grateful to my editor, Michael Tizzano, whose sharp eye and thoughtful guidance made this book stronger and more focused.

To my cover designer and typographer, Jasmine Hromjak, thank you for bringing this book to life with your creativity and skill.

To my mother, Melissa Passmore Williams, whose strength and faith through life's challenges inspire me and keep me moving forward.

Finally, thank you to every reader. This book exists because of you.

www.ingramcontent.com/pod-product-compliance
Lightning Source LLC
Chambersburg PA
CBHW061709120626
46550CB00003B/1151